# BIOGRAPHIC
# TESLA

# BIOGRAPHIC
# TESLA

**BRIAN CLEGG**

AMMONITE
PRESS

First published 2018 by
Ammonite Press
an imprint of Guild of Master Craftsman Publications Ltd
Castle Place, 166 High Street, Lewes, East Sussex, BN7 1XU,
United Kingdom
www.ammonitepress.com

ISBN 978 1 78145 353 7

Publisher: Jason Hook
Concept Design: Matt Carr
Design & Illustration: Matt Carr & Robin Shields
Editor: Jamie Pumfrey

Colour reproduction by GMC Reprographics
Printed and bound in Turkey

# CONTENTS

# ICONOGRAPHIC

WHEN WE CAN RECOGNIZE A SCIENTIST BY A SET OF ICONS, WE CAN ALSO RECOGNIZE HOW COMPLETELY THAT SCIENTIST AND THEIR WORK HAVE ENTERED OUR CULTURE AND OUR CONSCIOUSNESS.

# INTRODUCTION

Few other engineers or scientists have been as controversial as Nikola Tesla. Born in the Croatian village of Smiljan (then part of the Austrian Empire) in 1856, Tesla was both a genius and an eccentric. His engineering capabilities were second to none, but his technical successes came despite a frequent inability to accept scientific theory.

Tesla dropped out of the Austrian Polytechnic in Graz without completing his degree. After a short stint working in Budapest, he moved to Paris to take up the job that transformed his life, as an electrical engineer at the Société Electrique Edison. Two years later, the American manager in Paris was summoned to the USA and he took Tesla with him.

## "ERE LONG INTELLIGENCE – TRANSMITTED WITHOUT WIRES – WILL THROB THROUGH THE EARTH LIKE A PULSE THROUGH A LIVING ORGANISM."

—Nikola Tesla, lecture delivered before the Institution of Electrical Engineers, London, February 1892

After six months with the Edison Illuminating Company in New York, Tesla found backing to set up his own company. It lasted a year before collapsing, but in that time Tesla began to develop the ideas that would make him famous. American inventor Thomas Alva Edison used a direct current (DC) electricity supply. The competing alternating current (AC) system was much better for distribution, and was fine for lighting, but couldn't drive electric motors. Tesla developed the first practical AC motor, making AC far more attractive.

Tesla's design was licensed by Westinghouse, an Edison competitor. Although progress was slow, Westinghouse paid Tesla enough to enable him to set up his own lab in 1889 and work independently. It was around this time, after seeing German physicist Heinrich Hertz's experiments on electromagnetic waves, that he developed the Tesla coil. This produced high-voltage, high-frequency electricity, enabling him to use electrical induction to power light bulbs without a connection to the mains.

In 1891, Tesla became a US citizen and he began his most active phase. Despite a setback in 1895, when his lab burned down, he was involved in early experiments with X-rays and demonstrated a model radio-controlled boat. But he had a far bigger goal: transmitting electrical power without wires. Tesla's grand design would also enable worldwide communications. This was around the time that Guglielmo Marconi was developing radio. But despite later claiming that Marconi stole his ideas – and Marconi did infringe some Tesla patents – Tesla dismissed radio, both failing to grasp the theory of electromagnetism and feeling that the technology was too short-range to be practical.

Instead, Tesla envisaged electrical waves sent through the Earth, then returned through the air to complete the circuit. By 1904, he had constructed a huge 187ft (57m) transmitting tower at Wardenclyffe on Long Island in New York. This drained both Tesla's finances and those of his backers, without practical outcome. Although he struggled on until 1915, the project collapsed, Tesla's mortgages were foreclosed and the tower was sold for scrap.

Tesla continued to invent things, including a bladeless turbine, but his career lost impetus. For years he had lived in luxury hotels and continued to do so until his death in 1943, occasionally changing location as debts caught up with him. In later years, his best-known companions were pigeons, which he fed and encouraged into his rooms.

There is no doubt of Tesla's greatness as an engineer, which resulted in the unit of magnetic flux density being named after him, yet many of his claims verged on fantasy. He remains, to this day, a fascinating character.

"OF ALL THE FRICTIONAL RESISTANCES, THE ONE THAT MOST RETARDS HUMAN MOVEMENT IS IGNORANCE."

—Nikola Tesla,
*The Century*, 1900

# NIKOLA TESLA

## 01
## LIFE

"THE SCIENTISTS FROM FRANKLIN TO MORSE WERE CLEAR THINKERS AND DID NOT PRODUCE ERRONEOUS THEORIES. THE SCIENTISTS OF TODAY THINK DEEPLY INSTEAD OF CLEARLY. ONE MUST BE SANE TO THINK CLEARLY, BUT ONE CAN THINK DEEPLY AND BE QUITE INSANE."

—Nikola Tesla, *Modern Mechanics and Inventions*, 1934

# NIKOLA TESLA

## was born on 10 July 1856 in Smiljan – then in the Austrian Empire, now in Croatia

Born into an ethnic Serbian family, Tesla and his siblings lived in the inland village of Smiljan with his mother Đuka and his father Milutin, who was the local Orthodox priest. Tesla would later claim he got some of his practical ability and impressive memory from his mother. His older brother Dane was killed falling from a horse when Tesla was seven. Tesla also had two older sisters, Milka and Angelina, and one younger, Marica. Shortly after Dane's death, following Milutin to a new parish, the family moved to Gospić, a much larger town just 4 miles (7km) away.

It is often reported that Tesla was born during a storm with lightning striking the ground around the family. Given what followed it's a nice story, but it's never been proven to be anything more than that.

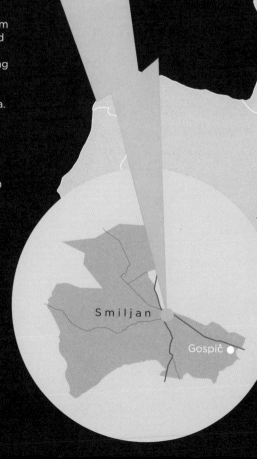

Smiljan

Gospić ●

CROATIA

Smiljan

Also born
in Smiljan:

# FERDINAND KOVAČEVIĆ

(1838–1913)
engineer and
telegraphic pioneer

## IOWA, USA

The first railroad bridge to cross the Mississippi River opens.

## LONDON, ENGLAND

Queen Victoria institutes the Victoria Cross to honour acts of valour.

## WASHINGTON, D.C., USA

Democrat James Buchanan is elected president.

## LONDON, ENGLAND

The National Portrait Gallery opens.

# THE WORLD IN 1856

## LONDON, ENGLAND

Mauveine, the first synthetic organic dye, is produced by William H. Perkin, starting the industrial chemical industry.

## FLORENCE, ITALY

Giovanni Caselli produces a prototype of the pantelegraph, the earliest form of fax machine.

The Tesla family had moved to the Austrian Empire back in the 1690s, during the Great Turkish War – a series of conflicts between the Ottoman Empire on one side, and the Hapsburg Empire, Poland-Lithuania, Venice and Russia on the other. Though of Serbian ancestry, Tesla and his family were well-rooted in what is now Croatia, on the south-western borders of the Austrian Empire. They still retained their own culture, though – for example, worshipping in Serbian Orthodox churches rather than Austrian Catholic ones. Under Austrian law, as the region was a military frontier, Tesla was enlisted as a baby into the First Lika Regiment and expected to take up active service at the age of 15.

## PARIS, FRANCE

The Treaty of Paris is signed, marking the end of the Crimean War.

## NEANDER VALLEY, GERMANY

The first fossils to be identified as *Homo neanderthalis* are dug up.

## NEPAL

Peak XV (later named Mount Everest) is designated the world's highest summit at 29,002ft (8,840m).

## CHINA

The Second Opium War with Western countries begins.

## PARIS, FRANCE

The Paris Declaration ends privateering on the high seas.

## HERAT, AFGHANISTAN

Persia's attempt to take the city of Herat sparks the Anglo-Persian war.

## CHRISTCHURCH, NEW ZEALAND

Christchurch becomes a city.

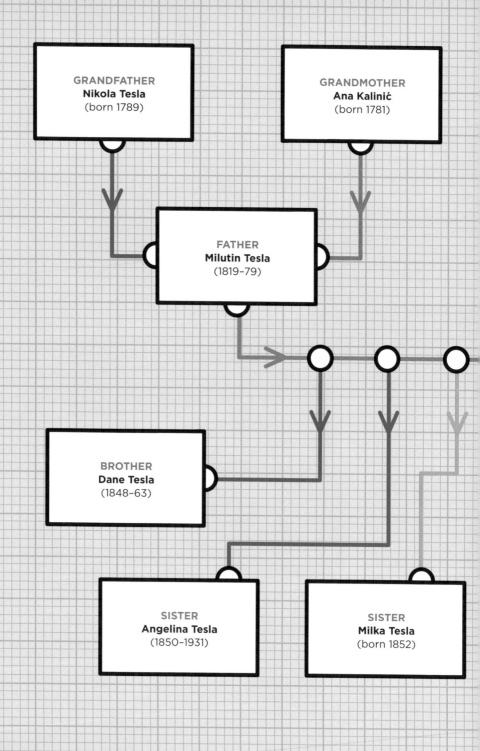

GRANDFATHER
**Nikola Tesla**
(born 1789)

GRANDMOTHER
**Ana Kalinić**
(born 1781)

FATHER
**Milutin Tesla**
(1819–79)

BROTHER
**Dane Tesla**
(1848–63)

SISTER
**Angelina Tesla**
(1850–1931)

SISTER
**Milka Tesla**
(born 1852)

## TESLA'S FAMILY TREE

**GRANDFATHER**
**Nikola Mandić**
(1800–63)

**GRANDMOTHER**
**Soka Budisavljević**
(born 1800)

**MOTHER**
**Georgina 'Đuka' Mandić**
(1822–92)

**Nikola Tesla**
(1856–1943)

**SISTER**
**Marica Tesla**
(1859–1938)

The family name Tesla refers to a small axe with a blade at right angles to the handle, which led to it being used as a nickname for people with protruding teeth; this could be the reason the family adopted it. Tesla's grandfather, Nikola, had been a soldier and his sons Milutin and Josif were expected to become officers. However, Milutin found military school difficult and left to enrol in a Serbian Orthodox seminary. He married Đuka Mandić, daughter of a priest from Gračac. Milutin's first posting was a coastal hamlet named Senj, before moving to Smiljan in 1852. Tesla was born four years later.

# EARLY LIFE

Tesla initially had a happy home life and seemed particularly close to his mother. He would later describe her as a great inventor who was excellent with her hands. However, he did seem to have some early mental issues, describing how on hearing an object mentioned he would see it so clearly he could not distinguish it from reality. Being an eyewitness to his brother's death when Tesla was only seven did not help. He disliked his new home in Gospić and when he found solace in books, his father tried to stop him reading. However, school and technical college would spark his imagination.

## 1874

Tesla's parents hide him in the mountains to avoid conscription in the Austro-Hungarian army.

## 1870

After recovering from serious illness, Tesla attends the gymnasium (high school) in Karlovac, 93 miles (150km) from home. He boards with his aunt and uncle.

## 1856

Nikola Tesla is born at midnight between 9 and 10 July at his parent's home in Smiljan.

## 1863

Tesla witnesses his older brother Dane die in a horse-riding accident.

## 1863

The Tesla family move to the town of Gospić where Nikola attends elementary school and the equivalent of junior high school.

## 1875

Tesla enters the Joanneum Polytechnic School in Graz. He receives a scholarship on the condition that he undertakes eight years of military service on graduation.

## 1877

Inspired by electrical devices, Tesla switches course to engineering, but his attendance drops off as he spends more time socializing and gambling than working.

## 1878

Tesla drops out of university and moves to Maribor, taking a job as an engineering draughtsman.

## 1879

Tesla's father Milutin dies.

MILUTIN TESLA 1819–1879

## 1882

Tesla moves to Paris to join the Edison company.

## 1881

Short of cash, Tesla moves to Budapest where he finds electrical engineering work.

## 1880

Tesla moves to Prague with the hope of starting a degree course at the university.

# UNUSUAL BEHAVIOUR

Tesla's early vision-like experiences and frequent illnesses grew into complex behavioural issues. Starting soon after his brother's death, they intensified as he got older. Some had a logical origin. He described how a scientist had shown him through a microscope the many organisms in the untreated Croatian drinking water. He wrote, "If you would watch only for a few minutes the horrible creatures, hairy and ugly beyond anything you could conceive, tearing each other up with the juices diffusing throughout the water – you would never again drink a drop of unboiled or unsterilized water." Others, such as his aversion to pearls, he could not explain.

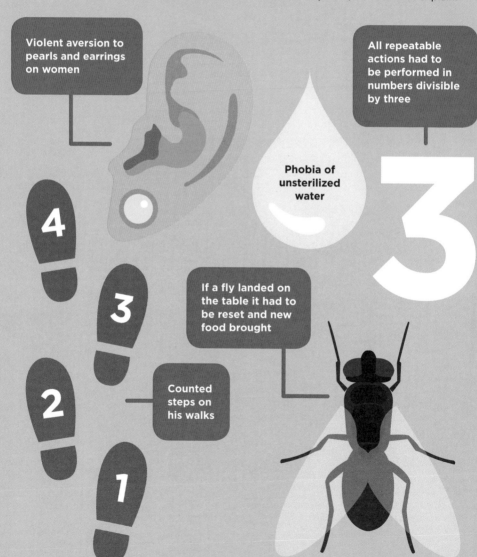

Violent aversion to pearls and earrings on women

All repeatable actions had to be performed in numbers divisible by three

Phobia of unsterilized water

If a fly landed on the table it had to be reset and new food brought

Counted steps on his walks

4

3

2

1

3

Avoided
handshakes

Hotel staff had to stay a minimum of 3ft (1m) away

No one else was allowed to use his table in the hotel dining room

Refused to touch other people's hair

Did not enjoy food unless he calculated the cubical contents of soup plates, coffee cups and pieces of food

# ADULTHOOD

Tesla's move to work for the Edison company in Paris would prove to be the starting point for a remarkable new life in the USA. After a brief stint with Edison in New York, Tesla branched out on his own, and though he would be involved with a range of companies and financiers, he would never again be just an employee. In the USA he seemed to develop a second persona. While there was still the reserved, highly inventive engineer, Tesla began to relish a position as a showman, demonstrating his electrical devices with a maximum emphasis on high-voltage displays, ideally passed through his own body.

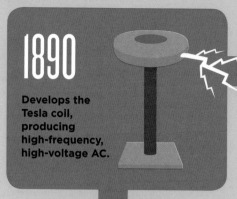

## 1890
Develops the Tesla coil, producing high-frequency, high-voltage AC.

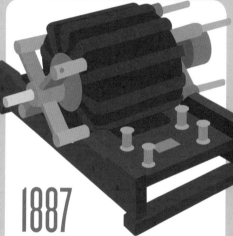

## 1887
Develops arguably his greatest invention, an alternating current (AC) induction motor based on a rotating magnetic field.

## 1884
Emigrates to the USA to work for Edison in New York.

## 1885
Sets up Tesla Electric Light and Manufacturing with Robert Lane and Benjamin Vail. The company collapses within the year.

# 1891

Becomes a
US citizen.

# 1943

Dies in The New
Yorker hotel from
a heart attack.

# 1893
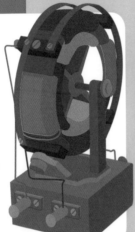

Advises the
Niagara Falls
Cataract
Construction
Company on
the use of two-
phase AC.

# 1915

As funds dry up, and with no
evidence of working technology,
Wardenclyffe is foreclosed.

# 1902

Moves to new
broadcast
power site at
Wardenclyffe,
Long Island.

# 1895

A fire destroys Tesla's South Fifth
Avenue laboratory.

# 1898

Demonstrates
a radio-
controlled boat.

# 1899

Establishes the first experimental
site for broadcast power at
Colorado Springs.

# A LOVE FOR PIGEONS

Tesla had relatively few friends, though some, notably the American couple Robert and Katharine Johnson, were very close. There is considerable debate about Tesla's sexuality. He said he had fallen in love in Smiljan, for the only time in his life, with a girl called Anna. He later argued that inventors didn't have time for love. There is some evidence that he was homosexual. He was clearly attracted to some men, and, though this may have been platonic, there was talk of his behaviour having caused a stir at the American Institute of Electrical Engineers. One thing is certain, though – Tesla loved pigeons.

Pigeons have

# 10,000

feathers

—**Nikola Tesla, interview with**
*New York World*, **1926**

"SOMETIMES I FEEL THAT BY NOT MARRYING I MADE TOO GREAT A SACRIFICE TO MY WORK, SO I HAVE DECIDED TO LAVISH ALL THE AFFECTION OF A MAN NO LONGER YOUNG ON THE FEATHERY TRIBE ... TO CARE FOR THOSE HOMELESS, HUNGRY OR SICK BIRDS IS THE DELIGHT OF MY LIFE."

Pigeons are able to distinguish ultraviolet rays

Speed of the fastest racing pigeon

mph

## DAILY ROUTINE

Tesla took daily walks to feed pigeons, fed them from his hotel window and looked after injured and sick birds in his room.

## EDISON MEDAL

When Tesla was due to receive the Edison Medal in 1917 he disappeared and was found feeding pigeons in Bryant Park.

## COMPLAINTS

Tesla frequently received complaints from the hotels he stayed in because he was keeping too many pigeons in his room.

## 1 BILLION
pigeons in the world

# 300
different species of pigeon

$2,000 The amount Tesla claimed to have spent on caring for a pigeon with a broken wing and leg, He even made a special device to support it.

# MONEY, MONEY, MONEY

 Tesla's earnings

 Investments in Tesla

 Tesla's debts

$450,000
$425,000
$400,000
$375,000
$350,000
$325,000
$300,000
$275,000
$250,000
$225,000
$200,000
$175,000
$150,000
$125,000
$100,000
$75,000
$50,000
$25,000

**$3,000**

**$88,000**

**$47,000**

**$100,000**

**$216,600**

| 1887 | 1888 | 1891 | 1895 | 1897 |
|------|------|------|------|------|
| Tesla's salary | 10-year contract for electric motor patents from Westinghouse | Amount received before the contract was torn up | From Edward Dean Adams to develop the Nikola Tesla Company | Paid by Westinghouse for Tesla patents |

In his youth, Tesla lived through financial difficulties, but when he reached the USA his relationship to finance became problematic. Briefly wealthy when he began to make money on his AC motor patents, Tesla moved from an apartment to a smart hotel – and lived in hotels for the rest of his life. Latterly, this was achieved by simply ignoring hotel bills and moving to a new location when the complaints became too loud. Remarkably, perhaps due to his public profile, none seemed inclined to sue. At the same time, he was dealing with financiers such as J. P. Morgan in business contracts worth hundreds of thousands of dollars.

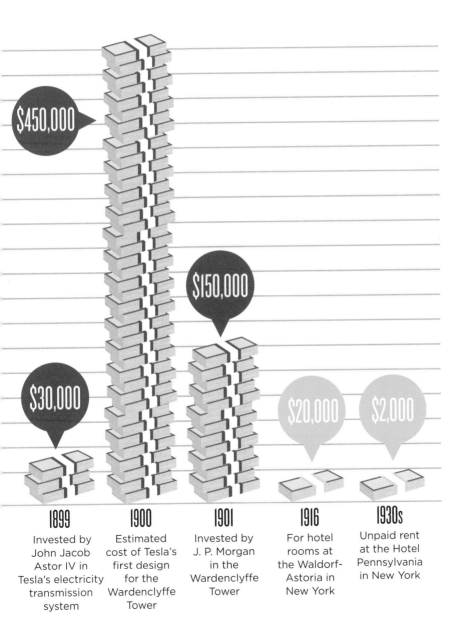

$30,000

$450,000

$150,000

$20,000

$2,000

| 1899 | 1900 | 1901 | 1916 | 1930s |
|---|---|---|---|---|
| Invested by John Jacob Astor IV in Tesla's electricity transmission system | Estimated cost of Tesla's first design for the Wardenclyffe Tower | Invested by J. P. Morgan in the Wardenclyffe Tower | For hotel rooms at the Waldorf-Astoria in New York | Unpaid rent at the Hotel Pennsylvania in New York |

# TESLA'S DEATH

In 1937, Tesla was hit by a taxi on a New York street and, despite being badly injured, refused hospital treatment. He never fully recovered. Between 1940 and 1942 he restricted his always limited diet even more, cutting down to boiled vegetables and then just warm milk. By 1942, Tesla's health was in serious decline and he seemed to be suffering the onset of dementia, once sending a messenger to deliver $100 to Mark Twain, who had died more than 30 years previously. He died in his sleep at The New Yorker hotel, having spent the last two days of his life alone in his hotel room. More than 2,000 mourners attended his funeral on 12 January at the Cathedral of St. John the Divine, New York.

## DATE:
### 7 JANUARY 1943

## AGE:
### 86

## CAUSE OF DEATH:
### CORONARY THROMBOSIS OR HEART ATTACK

## TESLA'S BOX

Tesla left a box at the Governor Clinton hotel, as collateral for the $400 he owed them. He claimed it contained a death ray and would explode if opened by an unauthorized individual. Scientist John Trump, Donald Trump's uncle, cautiously opened the box to discover it only contained a Wheatstone bridge – a simple electrical component.

"THE PRESIDENT AND I ARE DEEPLY SORRY TO HEAR OF THE DEATH OF MR NIKOLA TESLA. WE ARE GRATEFUL FOR HIS CONTRIBUTION TO SCIENCE AND INDUSTRY AND TO THIS COUNTRY."

Eleanor Roosevelt, 1943

Tesla's ashes were transported to Belgrade, Serbia, where they are held in a gold-plated sphere at the Nikola Tesla Museum.

# NIKOLA TESLA

## 02
### WORLD

"IF EDISON HAD A NEEDLE TO FIND IN A HAYSTACK, HE WOULD PROCEED AT ONCE WITH THE DILIGENCE OF THE BEE TO EXAMINE STRAW AFTER STRAW UNTIL HE FOUND THE OBJECT OF HIS SEARCH ... I WAS A SORRY WITNESS OF SUCH DOINGS, KNOWING THAT A LITTLE THEORY AND CALCULATION WOULD HAVE SAVED HIM 90 PER CENT OF HIS LABOR."

—Nikola Tesla, *The New York Times,* 1931

# EARLY ELECTRICITY

English scientist Michael Faraday's invention of the electrical generator took electricity from a dramatic showpiece with little application to something that industries and homes could use. But before this could happen, power had to be generated and distributed. Initially, a plethora of companies set up their own systems – often there were many with different standards in the same city. The first domestic use of electricity was lighting. Once English inventor and physicist Joseph Swan developed a practical light bulb, soon followed by Thomas Edison in the US, the benefits of electric lights over gas soon became clear. But it would only be as standards emerged that large-scale deployment would become possible.

1884 7.5kW

1889 75kW

1892 100kW

1893 120kW

1894 150kW

1898 1,000kW

1901 1,500kW

1905 3,500kW

1908 6,000kW

1912 25,000kW

TYPICAL TURBINE GENERATOR SIZE

# 1907 ELECTRICITY SUPPLY STATISTICS

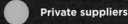 Municipal suppliers

Private suppliers

UK    US

**233**

**156**

**3,426**

**1,252**

**75%**
of UK suppliers had fewer than 1,000 customers

**2** UK suppliers had 10,000 customers or more

**26** UK suppliers had fewer than 100 customers

**33** suppliers in London

# WORKING FOR EDISON

Although Tesla did not work for Edison for long – he joined the French branch of the company in 1882 and left the US arm at the start of 1885 – there is no doubt Edison and his ability to turn inventing prowess into commercial success had a huge influence on Tesla. While Tesla was far better educated and belittled Edison's '1% inspiration, 99% perspiration' approach, he would never have Edison's ability to capitalize on his inventions.

## EDISON'S INVENTIONS:

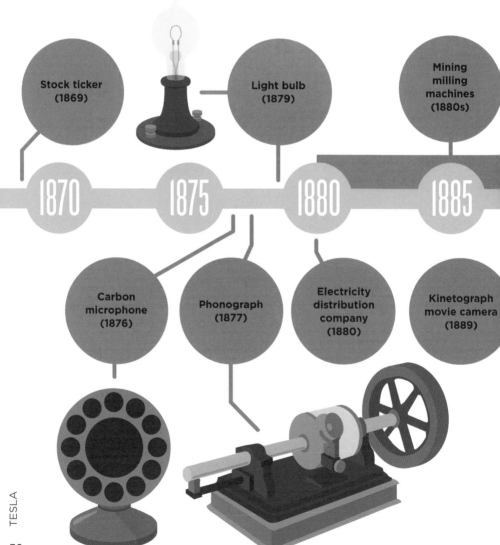

Stock ticker (1869)

Light bulb (1879)

Mining milling machines (1880s)

1870

1875

1880

1885

Carbon microphone (1876)

Phonograph (1877)

Electricity distribution company (1880)

Kinetograph movie camera (1889)

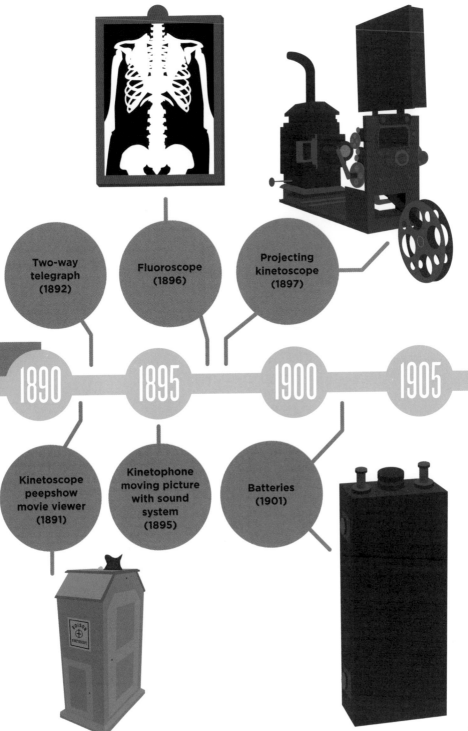

Two-way telegraph (1892)

Fluoroscope (1896)

Projecting kinetoscope (1897)

1890 1895 1900 1905

Kinetoscope peepshow movie viewer (1891)

Kinetophone moving picture with sound system (1895)

Batteries (1901)

# TESLA'S NEW YORK

Tesla lived in New York from 1884 to his death in 1943. During that time, the city underwent a transformation worthy of Tesla's engineering ingenuity. Its population boomed. Initially, used to a more cosmopolitan European style, Tesla found New York brash and unfriendly. He wrote, "What I had left was beautiful, artistic and fascinating in every way; what I saw here was machined, rough and unattractive ... 'Is this America?' I asked myself in painful surprise. 'It is a century behind Europe in civilization.'" However, in time he came to love New York's energy and 'anything's possible' attitude.

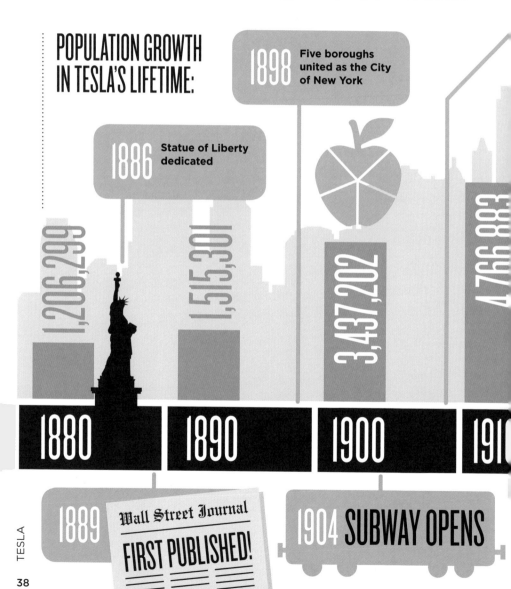

## POPULATION GROWTH IN TESLA'S LIFETIME:

**1898** Five boroughs united as the City of New York

**1886** Statue of Liberty dedicated

1,206,299

1,515,301

3,437,202

4,766,883

**1880**

**1890**

**1900**

**1910**

**1889** *Wall Street Journal* FIRST PUBLISHED!

**1904** SUBWAY OPENS

**1909** Manhattan Bridge connecting Manhattan to Brooklyn opens

**1931** Empire State Building opens

**1930** Chrysler Building opens

**1932** Radio City Music Hall opens

5,620,048

6,930,446

7,454,995

**1920**

**1930**

**1940**

**1913** Grand Central station opens

# LET THERE BE LIGHT

In 1893, The World's Fair, celebrating the 400th anniversary of Christopher Columbus's arrival in America, was held in Chicago, USA. The exposition, designed to showcase achievements of nations across the world, covered more than 600 acres of the city, and was attended by more than 27 million people during its six-month run. The scale and grandeur of the event far exceeded previous fairs, and it became a symbol of American progress.

One of the 14 "great buildings" (each one showcasing a particular speciality) was the Electricity Building, devoted solely to electrical exhibits. To supply power to the building and provide lighting to the fair, Edison General Electric offered direct current at a cost of $1.8m. Tesla, through Westinghouse Electric, countered with an offer to supply an alternating current system at a third of the price. Knowing the importance of the fair, Edison proposed reducing their costs to $554,000, but Westinghouse once again undercut them at $399,000. It was a historic moment for Tesla and Westinghouse.

"THE FAIR ALONE CONSUMED THREE TIMES AS MUCH ELECTRICITY AS THE ENTIRE CITY OF CHICAGO. THESE WERE IMPORTANT ENGINEERING MILESTONES, BUT WHAT VISITORS ADORED WAS THE SHEER BEAUTY OF SEEING SO MANY LIGHTS IGNITED IN ONE PLACE, AT ONE TIME. EVERY BUILDING, INCLUDING THE MANUFACTURERS AND LIBERAL ARTS BUILDING, WAS OUTLINED IN WHITE BULBS."

—Erik Larson, *The Devil in the White City*, 2003

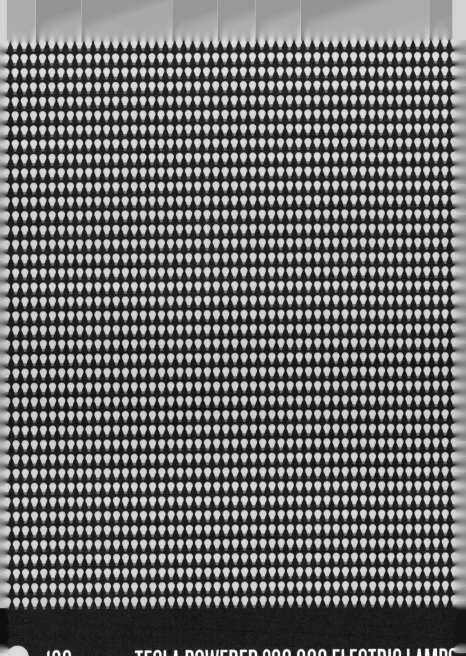

 = 100    TESLA POWERED 200,000 ELECTRIC LAMPS

# TIMELINE TO TESLA'S MOTOR

The vast majority of Tesla's inventions were electrical in nature – the whole concept of electricity and its uses appealed to both the engineer and the showman in him. While Tesla's designs for electric motors were sophisticated feats of engineering, his public and private shows – where he entertained the likes of Mark Twain – were flamboyant displays. He would send artificial lightning bolts across the room and light lamps wirelessly or using current conducted through his body. This mix showed the degree to which Tesla was transitional, from the early regard of electricity as primarily an entertainment to it becoming the essential power supply of the world.

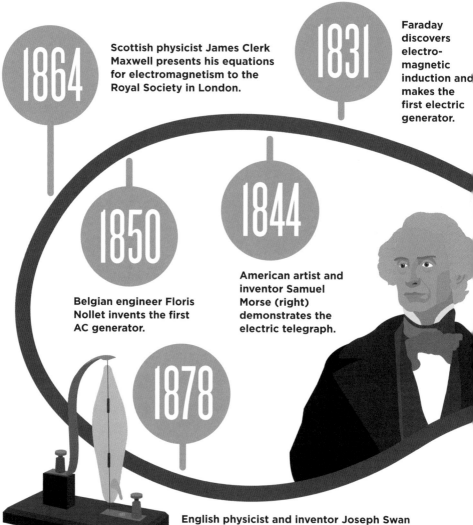

**1864**
Scottish physicist James Clerk Maxwell presents his equations for electromagnetism to the Royal Society in London.

**1831**
Faraday discovers electro-magnetic induction and makes the first electric generator.

**1850**
Belgian engineer Floris Nollet invents the first AC generator.

**1844**
American artist and inventor Samuel Morse (right) demonstrates the electric telegraph.

**1878**
English physicist and inventor Joseph Swan produces a practical electric light bulb (left).

## 600 BCE

Static electricity from materials such as amber is noted by the Ancient Greek philosopher Thales.

## 1600

English natural philosopher William Gilbert uses the terms 'electrical' and 'electrica' for the first time. They are derived from Latin *electricus*, meaning 'amber-like'.

## 1720s

English natural philosopher Stephen Gray discovers the flow of electricity, conductors and insulators.

## 1820

Danish scientist Hans Christian Ørsted (left) discovers a relationship between electricity and magnetism.

## 1800

Italian scientist Alessandro Volta invents the electric cell.

## 1827

German scientist Georg Ohm describes electrical resistance.

## 1821

English scientist Michael Faraday makes a simple electric motor.

## 1887

Tesla files a patent for his AC motor (right).

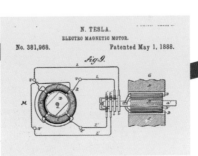

N. TESLA.
ELECTRO MAGNETIC MOTOR.
No. 381,968.          Patented May 1, 1888.
*Fig.9.*

# X-RAY SPECS

In 1894, Tesla noticed that some photographic plates had become spoiled without ever being exposed to light. The plates had been left near Geissler and Crookes tubes (glass tubes with high voltages passed through a near vacuum). Tesla did not investigate further, but in 1896 heard of Wilhelm Röntgen's discovery of X-rays. It seems that, unawares, Tesla had observed them, as several others had earlier. Tesla coils (see page 58) were ideal for producing the high voltages required to generate powerful X-rays and Tesla was soon producing quality X-ray images, but he decided not to get into the field as the production of vacuum tubes was too specialist.

## 56

## Ba

### 137.327

## BARIUM

**Used to make the gut visible in X-rays.**

## DNA DISCOVERY

**X-rays were used to unravel the structure of DNA.**

## ART

**X-rays have been used to reveal the secrets of what's under the top coat of paintings by artists such as Van Gogh and Leonardo da Vinci.**

## X-RAY SPACE

**Material falling into black holes gives off X-rays.**

# X-RAY FIRSTS:

**1785** — William Morgan first notices the effect (though not the cause) in London, England.

**1886** — The fogging of sealed photographic plates by discharge tubes is observed by Ivan Pulyui in Prague, Czech Republic.

**1895** — This time on purpose, Wilhelm Röntgen takes an X-ray image of his wife's hand, wearing a ring.

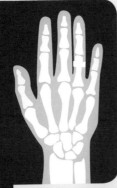

**1895** — In Munich, Germany, Wilhelm Röntgen accidentally X-rays his hand while moving a sample.

**1896** — John Hall-Edwards takes an X-ray for medical purposes – a patient with a needle stuck in their hand – in Birmingham, England.

**1914** — Marie Curie utilizes mobile X-ray vehicles in the First World War.

**1896** — In New Hampshire, USA, Gilman Frost makes X-rays of broken bones.

**1912** — Max von Laue, with Paul Knipping and Walter Friedrich, uses X-rays in the study of crystals (later used for the structure of DNA) in Zurich, Switzerland.

WORLD

45

## COLORADO SPRINGS

### $30,000

First payment from $100,000 total promised by John Jacob Astor IV to fund the Colorado Springs lab. The remaining $70,000 is never paid.

### POWER SOURCE

Colorado Springs streetcar line

> "SIGNALING TO MARS? I HAVE APPARATUS WHICH CAN ACCOMPLISH IT BEYOND ANY QUESTION."

—Nikola Tesla,
*Times-Herald,*
1899

### 50 MILLION VOLTS

Voltage claimed for the magnifying transmitter

### 60ft (18m)

Distance at which Tesla powered bulbs from his transmitter

142ft (43m) MAST

### LONGEST CLAIMED REACH: 1 MILE*

### 1,800 MILES (2,900km)
DISTANCE FROM NEW YORK CITY

*Distance Tesla claimed he transmitted power, but only Tesla himself witnessed this.

# TO WARDENCLYFFE

A major part of Tesla's life was spent on a project designed to broadcast power to any location on Earth, which also promised near-instant communications. Wireless telegraphy was the hot new topic, with experimental radio being developed. But Tesla thought radio too weak and slow. He proposed using electric waves, tuned to the resonant frequency of the Earth and completing the circuit through the air. Scientifically this made little sense, but Tesla set up experimental stations first at Colorado Springs and then at Wardenclyffe, on Long Island, where hundreds of thousands of dollars were invested in equipment that he always claimed was on the verge of working.

## FUNDING

**$150,000 from J. P. Morgan for 51% of patent rights from Wardenclyffe (Tesla asked for a preliminary extra payment of $25,000 but it was refused); $33,000 as a personal investment by Tesla; $10,000 raised on Wardenclyffe mortgage (later foreclosed).**

## 200 KILOWATTS
**Magnifying transmitter planned power output**

## LONGEST CLAIMED REACH: AUSTRALIA

## 65 MILES (105km)
DISTANCE FROM NEW YORK CITY

187ft (57m) BROADCAST TOWER

# FREE ENERGY AND CONSPIRACIES

The internet is rife with conspiracy theorists, convinced that vested interests suppressed Tesla's amazing inventions. These are typically 'free energy' devices, supposedly invented by Tesla. Such devices use rotating discs within a mix of coils and magnets and are said to produce more electricity than they use. This makes them perpetual motion machines, which can't work under the laws of physics. Some claim they use zero-point energy, which exists but can't be used as it is, by definition, the lowest level of energy. Tesla never claimed to produce free energy, but his name is always attached: this typifies Tesla's mix of the practical with irreproducible claims. Instead, Tesla planned for wireless energy distribution, with the intention of selling receivers for wireless telegraphy and providing the energy at a cost.

## "NO FREE ENERGY DEVICE WILL EVER BE ALLOWED TO REACH THE MARKET."

—Nikola Tesla

## AMOUNT INVESTED TO ACHIEVE 'FREE ENERGY':

In 1901, J. P. Morgan invested

# $150,000

Morgan's investment is the modern equivalent of

# $4,370,000

in terms of commodities

Morgan's investment is the modern equivalent of

# $19,800,000

in terms of labour value (unskilled)

Morgan's investment is the modern equivalent of

# $34,500,000

in terms of labour value (production worker)

Tesla raised

# $33,000

by selling personal property

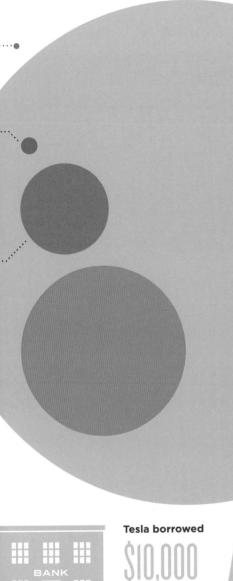

**Morgan's investment is the modern equivalent of**

# $124,000,000

**in terms of proportion of GDP**

**Tesla borrowed**

# $10,000

**from a bank**

**Tesla owed**

# $30,000

**to Westinghouse for equipment**

# 5 THINGS YOU DIDN'T KNOW ABOUT TESLA

**1** Edison attempted to discredit Tesla and Westinghouse's AC system by using it to electrocute animals, from a dog all the way up to an elephant, in spite of Tesla's correct assertion that direct current was more dangerous.

**2** Tesla grew up in the Austro-Hungarian Empire, where many different languages were spoken. Telsa learnt eight languages: Serbo-Croatian, English, Czech, German, French, Hungarian, Italian and Latin.

**3** Tesla's first great demonstration was the 'Egg of Columbus'. Inspired by the story that Columbus won the support of the Spanish court by promising to balance an egg on its end (by cracking it), Tesla used a rotating magnetic field to spin a copper-plated egg on its point.

**4** Tesla amassed an impressive collection of patents. The exact number is uncertain, but he was awarded 308 in a total of 27 countries.

**5** Tesla's favourite New York restaurant was Delmonico's, but as he grew older he restricted himself to very simple food and could not sample the restaurant's signature dishes of Lobster Newburg and Baked Alaska.

# NIKOLA TESLA

# 03
## WORK

# "INVENTION IS THE MOST IMPORTANT PRODUCT OF MAN'S CREATIVE BRAIN. THE ULTIMATE PURPOSE IS THE COMPLETE

# MASTERY OF MIND OVER THE MATERIAL WORLD, THE HARNESSING OF HUMAN NATURE TO HUMAN NEEDS."

—Nikola Tesla, *Electrical Experimenter*, 1919

# THE INDUCTION MOTOR

Tesla's greatest achievements were his alternating current (AC) motors. Contemporary direct current (DC) electric motors needed difficult-to-maintain brushes to carry current to the rotor, the rotating coils inside the motor. While in Budapest, Tesla had realized that if he could create a rotating magnetic field, it would induce currents in the rotor without the need for a connection. He first devised a multi-phase motor, where the rotating field was produced using different AC currents out of phase. But AC supply was often just single phase, on only two wires. To solve this, he developed a way to split the phase of the current, producing the same effect internally.

## MOTOR

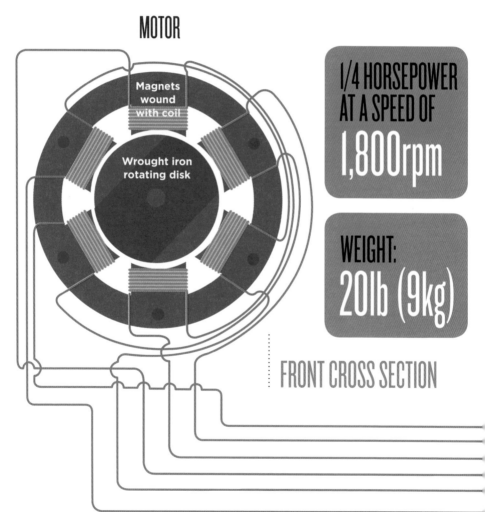

Magnets wound with coil

Wrought iron rotating disk

1/4 HORSEPOWER AT A SPEED OF

1,800rpm

WEIGHT: 20lb (9kg)

FRONT CROSS SECTION

# TESLA FILED 19 INDUCTION MOTOR PATENTS

**1888**
| | |
|---|---|
| 0381968 | Electro Magnetic Motor |
| 0381969 | Electro Magnetic Motor |
| 0382279 | Electro Magnetic Motor |

**1889**
| | |
|---|---|
| 0405858 | Electro Magnetic Motor |
| 0416191 | Electro Magnetic Motor |
| 0416193 | Electro Magnetic Motor |
| 0416194 | Electric Motor |
| 0416195 | Electro Magnetic Motor |
| 0418248 | Electro Magnetic Motor |

**1890**
| | |
|---|---|
| 0424036 | Electro Magnetic Motor |
| 0433700 | Alternating Current Electro Magnetic Motor |
| 0433701 | Alternating Current Motor |
| 0433703 | Electro Magnetic Motor |

**1891**
| | |
|---|---|
| 0445207 | Electro Magnetic Motor |
| 0455067 | Electro Magnetic Motor |
| 0459772 | Electro Magnetic Motor |
| 0464666 | Electro Magnetic Motor |

**1894**
| | |
|---|---|
| 0524426 | Electromagnetic Motor |

**1896**
| | |
|---|---|
| 0555190 | Alternating Motor |

**TESLA PATENT 0381968 (below)**

A diagramatic illustration of a motor and generator.

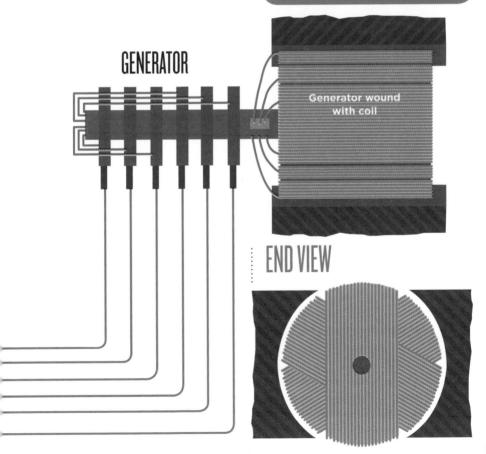

GENERATOR

Generator wound with coil

END VIEW

# AC OR DC?

In the early days of electrical supplies, it was not clear whether alternating current (AC) or direct current (DC) would become the standard. In the USA, Edison was dedicated to DC, while a number of competitors, notably Westinghouse, championed AC. Despite Tesla initially working for Edison, he was always convinced of the benefits of AC, and with his AC motor became Westinghouse's technical wizard. AC made it easy to change voltage through a simple transformer, and high voltages resulted in less loss of energy on long-distance transmission. But DC was initially appealing because DC motors were much easier to design.

Thomas Edison had built 121 DC power stations in the USA by 1887.

In 1886, Ganz Works, an electric company located in Budapest, electrified all of Rome with AC.

## DIFFERENT USES:

**SOLAR PANELS**

**BATTERIES**

**LEDS**

**CAR MOTORS**

**APPLIANCES**

**HOUSEHOLD SUPPLY**

0V

● DC – DIRECT CURRENT  ● AC – ALTERNATING CURRENT

In DC, a constant voltage is sent down the wire. Current always flows the same way.

In AC, the voltage oscillates up and down with current repeatedly changing direction.

# THE TESLA COIL

Tesla's development of the Tesla coil was driven by his work on radio waves. Early transmitters required a very fast set of electrical pulses to produce a spark and generate radio waves, but the devices used to achieve this were quite crude. The Tesla coil was a futuristic design that produced high voltage, high frequency AC electricity, and it was used for generating such electrical pulses until the 1920s. But Tesla decided radio was not an effective method for long distance communication – his ultimate goal. So, he used his coils instead for a range of other applications, including experiments in X-rays and the wireless powering of light bulbs. Today, the Tesla coil has little use apart from being a compact method for making pretty displays of electrical sparks.

## HOW IT WORKS

The Tesla coil consists of two parts: a primary coil and a secondary coil, connected by a spark gap – an air gap between two electrodes. A current is passed through the primary coil via a high-voltage transformer that steps up the voltage. This charges the high voltage (HV) capacitor. When it is sufficiently high enough, the charge jumps across the air between the spark gap and energy is transferred efficiently from the primary to the secondary coil. It is then stored in the torus to be released. Tesla added a high frequency output from an AC alternator. It modified the circuit so that it added a resonant boost to the voltage, and the result was a high frequency and voltage output.

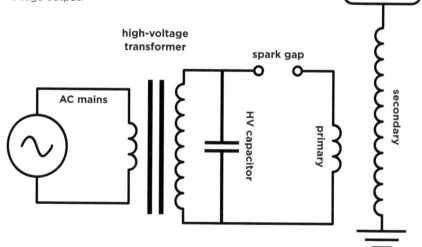

**20ft (6m)**
DIAMETER OF "RESONATOR" COIL

**30ft (9m)**
HEIGHT OF "RESONATOR" COIL

**135ft (41m)**
LENGTH OF "LIGHTNING BOLTS" PRODUCED

**300 kW**
INPUT POWER

**10m VOLTS**
GENERATED (AT 150 kHz)

## MAGNIFYING TRANSMITTER

In 1899, at his Colorado Springs laboratory, Tesla built a large modified version of a Tesla coil. With a diameter of more than 50 feet, he called it the "magnifying transmitter" and intended to use it to transmit power wirelessly to a distant receiver. Somewhat different from the classic two-coil Tesla coil, it included a third "resonator" coil (shown above) attached to the top of the secondary.

# WIRELESS LIGHTING

When Tesla was experimenting with his newly developed coil, he noticed that in some circumstances nearby Geissler tubes lit up. These were a form of lighting developed by the German physicist Heinrich Geissler back in 1857. The sealed tube, a forerunner of the neon light, had an electrode at each end and a low-pressure gas inside. When a high voltage was put across the electrodes, the tube glowed as electrons displaced from the gas atoms by the current dropped back in place and gave off photons. Convinced this would revolutionize lighting, Tesla developed increasingly dramatic demonstrations of wireless lighting.

NEON

XENON

COLOURS PRODUCE

MERCURY VAPOUR

OXYGEN

WATER
VAPOUR

HELIUM

KRYPTON

DIFFERENT GASES

HYDROGEN

ARGON

# THE OSCILLATOR

Given Tesla's impressive range of electrical inventions, it might seem surprising that one included a steam engine (admittedly as part of a new generator). AC generators were usually (and still are) a kind of back-to-front motor, where a coil is turned inside a magnetic field. This was fine for normal uses of electrical power, but Tesla's sensitive equipment suffered because the steam engine that powered the generator did not run at a totally constant speed, so the frequency of the AC varied. To get around this, he designed his 'oscillator', a reciprocating steam engine that produced steady, high-frequency output.

WEIGHT:
**1–2lb**
(454–907g)

PRESSURE:
**400psi**

STEAM TEMP: **200°C**

HEIGHT: 7 INCHES (18 CM)

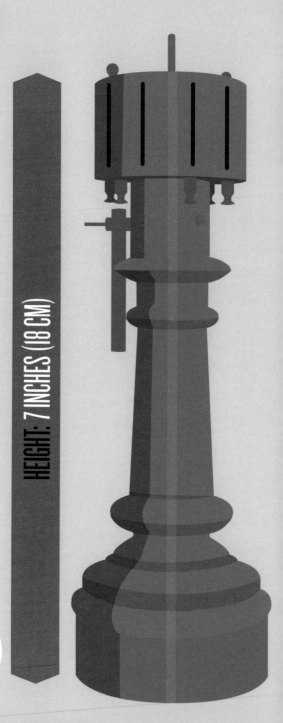

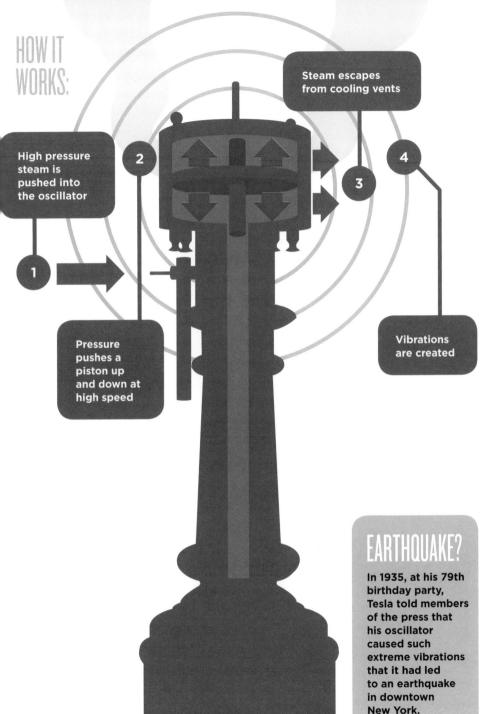

**High pressure steam is pushed into the oscillator**

**1**

**2**

**Pressure pushes a piston up and down at high speed**

**Steam escapes from cooling vents**

**3**

**4**

**Vibrations are created**

## EARTHQUAKE?

In 1935, at his 79th birthday party, Tesla told members of the press that his oscillator caused such extreme vibrations that it had led to an earthquake in downtown New York.

WORK

# HARNESSING NIAGARA

In 1892, Westinghouse decided to bid for the contract to provide electrical equipment to harness Niagara Falls. With expertise in locomotive brakes, Westinghouse had first suggested transmitting the power by compressed air. However, the Cataract Construction Company decided to go with electricity. Westinghouse bid with Tesla's polyphase system, combined with technology developed in-house that converted multiphase AC into single-phase AC or DC after transmission. Tesla, who claimed to have dreamed of harnessing Niagara as a child, offered himself as consultant to Dean Adams, head of the project. Surprisingly, Tesla recommended two-phase AC, rather than his usually preferred three-phase. Westinghouse won the contract.

FLOW:

**6** million cubic feet per minute (170,000 cubic metres per minute)

HIGHEST DROP: 167ft (51m)

LUNA ISLAND

AMERICAN FALLS

BRIDAL VEIL FALLS

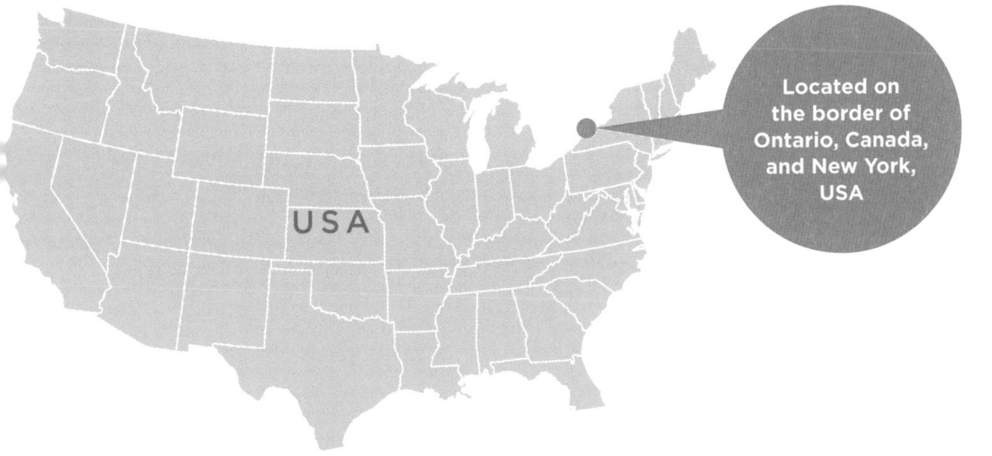

Located on the border of Ontario, Canada, and New York, USA

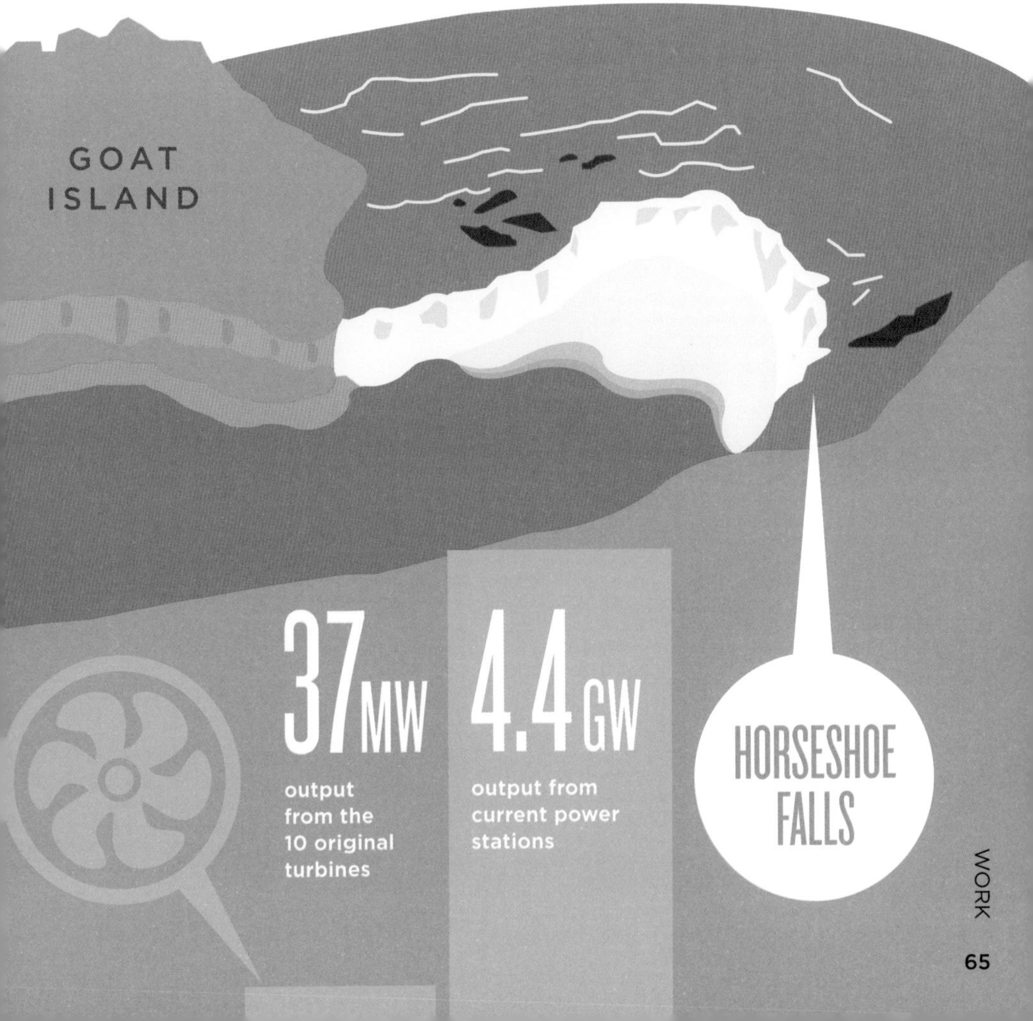

USA

GOAT ISLAND

**37**MW
output from the 10 original turbines

**4.4**GW
output from current power stations

HORSESHOE FALLS

Both Tesla and Edison came from poor backgrounds, but Edison had far fewer opportunities and was less culturally refined than Tesla. Their biggest difference was in education. Although Tesla did not graduate, he had covered both physics and electrical engineering to degree level. Edison's approach to invention was to rely on others for technical expertise and to try as many variants as possible in the hope of success. Tesla was far more likely to base his work on theory, which worked well for his AC work, but later proved a problem as his ideas diverged from the scientific consensus.

# NIKOLA TESLA

## 86

## FAMILY

**Was never married and had no known children.**

## BEST KNOWN INVENTIONS

**AC MOTOR**      **TESLA COIL**

## QUOTABILITY

**Making predictions of the wonders of future technology, from robots to mobile phones**

## BORN

**Smiljan, Austrian Empire (now in Croatia)**

## NIKOLA TESLA (1856 – 1943)

# THOMAS EDISON

## 84

## CHILDREN
A girl and two boys from each marriage.

## MARRIAGE
Mary Stilwell from 1871 to 1884 (deceased) and Mina Miller from 1886 to death.

## QUOTABILITY
Snappy quotes, often about perseverance and hard work

## BEST KNOWN INVENTIONS

LIGHT BULB          PHONOGRAPH

## BORN
Milan, Ohio, USA

# AHEAD OF HIS TIME

Frustratingly, Tesla occasionally started a project that was ahead of its time, only to drop it, primarily to concentrate on the dead end of wireless transmission of power. This was certainly the case with 'teleautomatics', his name for remotely controlled devices. His radio-controlled boat, a first in 1898, had an electric motor, steering, lighting and an explosive charge that could be controlled by a radio transmitter. The radio mechanism itself was not original – it used a receiver called a coherer devised in 1890 by French physicist Édouard Branly – but Tesla's aquatic predecessor to the drone certainly was.

**Tesla's use of phosphorescent lamps:**
1893

**Public use:**
1930s

**Tesla's radio-controlled boat:**
1898

**Available to the public:**
1940s

**Tesla's use of wireless electricity:**
1899

**Tesla's proposal for an instant communication handheld device:**
1902

**Tesla's concept for radar:**
1917

**Radar developed:**
1930s

TESLA

1890   1900   1910   1920   1930   1940   195

First long-distance wireless transfer (using microwaves):

# 1960s

Smartphone technology:

# 2000s

1960   1970   1980   1990   2000   2010   2020

# THE DEATH RAY?

Tesla famously left a 'death ray' in a box as surety for his hotel bill, only for it to turn out to be a commonplace electrical device. Yet he did put considerable effort into an electric weapon. This wasn't an electric wave device, but was intended to use electricity to propel a stream of particles at high speed from a source like a Van der Graaf generator. Like many of his later inventions, the particle beam weapon was never built – and it's not certain his device could give particles sufficient momentum or keep them in a tight beam – but he did produce detailed plans.

Would kill an army of

## 1 MILLION SOLDIERS

$25,000 — Funding Tesla asked of J. P. Morgan to produce a prototype (not provided)

$25,000 — Fee asked by Tesla of Soviet Russia for his plans (not paid)

$30m — Price of the system (presumably when working) as offered to British government (declined)

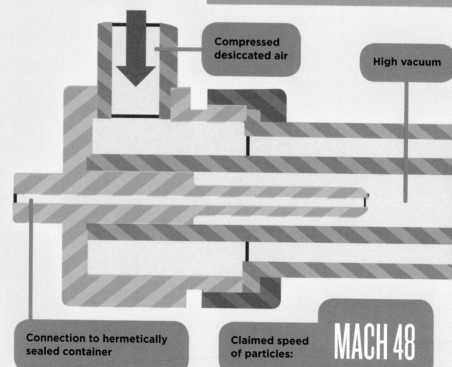

Compressed desiccated air

High vacuum

Connection to hermetically sealed container

Claimed speed of particles: **MACH 48**

Would bring down a fleet of

# 10,000 ENEMY AIRCRAFT

= 100 AIRCRAFT

# RANGE: 250 MILES (400km)

# 50 MILLION VOLTS

**Internal dynamic pressure**

**External static pressure**

# HOW IT WORKS

Tesla's proposed device used high voltage electricity to accelerate a jet of charged particles.

Speed of sound is Mach 1

# TRUE OR FALSE?

**INVENTED X-RAYS BEFORE RÖNTGEN**

**RECEIVED A SIGNAL FROM MARS**

**INVEN BLAD TUR**

He certainly made X-ray images soon after, but there is no evidence he achieved them earlier.

Claimed to have received a short repeating signal. Rather unlikely to have been from Mars.

**MADE THE FIRST RADIO-CONTROLLED BOAT**

True. He called the system teleautomatics.

...sla was responsible for a great many ...markable inventions, yet some of his ...aims – often unsubstantiated – stretch ...e belief to breaking point. From his ...ollege days, Tesla demonstrated an ...agination that was powerful – if ...constrained by practicality and physical ...ws. He dreamed up, for example, a ...draulic system to se...d mail through

undersea pipes between contin... a high-speed transport mechan... involved building a ring around ... equator, suspended so it could ... while the Earth whizzed past be... These, though, he never claimed... constructed. But his work ran th... from extraordinary inventions to... proven theories to false beliefs...

CLAIMED IT WOULD
TAKE SIX MONTHS
TO CONSTRUCT
EQUIPMENT THAT
COULD TRANSMIT
A WIRELESS
SIGNAL ACROSS
THE ATLANTIC

AND THAT IT
WOULD DELIVER
WORLDWIDE
WIRELESS
TELEGRAPHY

CLAIMED
TO HAVE
TRANSMITTED
POWER
WIRELESSLY
ACROSS TENS
OF MILES

Never
achieved.

Unproven.
No-one was
allowed to witness
it (including his
assistants).

PRODUCED
WAVES FOR USE
IN TRANSMITTING
ENERGY THAT
TRAVELLED FASTER
THAN LIGHT

DESIGNED A
PARTICLE BEAM
WEAPON

True, though it is
doubtful whether
it would have
worked.

INVENTED AN
IMPROVED CAR
SPEEDOMETER

INVENTED
A MOTOR
THAT RAN ON
COSMIC RAYS

20    30

10         40

0          50

True

False
claim

Tried
but failed

Unclear

# 5 THINGS YOU DIDN'T KNOW ABOUT TESLA'S WORK

**1** Confusing cause and effect, Tesla observed that a lightning flash was followed by a downpour and hoped one day to be able to control the weather using electricity.

**2** One of Tesla's more dramatic claims was that he had a pocket-sized version of the mechanical oscillator that could set up a sympathetic vibration so strong that it would bring down the Empire State Building. It was never demonstrated.

**3** In his experiments with X-rays, Tesla at first thought they were beneficial, but when he and his assistants received burns and started to have headaches, he realized that exposure needed to be limited.

**4** In the 1930s, Tesla built a mechanical oscillator connected to a platform. Standing on the platform, he and his assistants found the sensation pleasant, but then had to hurriedly rush to the toilet. Tesla believed the device speeded food through the intestines and so might help those with digestive ailments.

**5** Tesla's last working invention was a turbine that had no blades, but turned disks by drag as his AC motor pulled the rotor along. It worked, but couldn't match the efficiency of existing turbines. The design has been used in reverse as a pump.

# NIKOLA TESLA

## 04
# LEGACY

"EINSTEIN'S RELATIVITY WORK IS A MAGNIFICENT MATHEMATICAL GARB WHICH FASCINATES, DAZZLES AND MAKES PEOPLE BLIND TO THE UNDERLYING ERRORS. THE THEORY IS LIKE A BEGGAR CLOTHED IN PURPLE WHOM IGNORANT PEOPLE TAKE FOR A KING ... ITS EXPONENTS ARE BRILLIANT MEN BUT THEY ARE METAPHYSICISTS RATHER THAN SCIENTISTS."

—Nikola Tesla, *The New York Times*, 1935

# RECOGNITION

Tesla won many awards, though never the Nobel Prize, despite a mistaken announcement by *The New York Times* in 1915 that he was to share the physics prize with Edison. In 1931, journalist Kenneth Swezey organized a party to mark Tesla's 75th birthday. This became the first of a series of annual events at which Tesla was given the chance to announce his latest thinking to the public. Tesla was increasingly portrayed as a great mind, equivalent to Einstein. Over the years his ideas would take on a mythical status, with some followers convinced that every vague suggestion was a tested invention, suppressed by Tesla's opponents. As his legend grew, so did his trophy cabinet.

## 1894

**Elliott Cresson Medal of the Franklin Institute, Philadelphia, USA.**

## 1931

**Tesla appears on the cover of *Time* magazine.**

## 1934

**The John Scott Legacy Medal, from the city of Philadelphia, USA.**

## 1936

**Order of the White Eagle, I Class, awarded by the Government of Yugoslavia.**

## 1895

Order of Prince Danilo I awarded by the royal family of Montenegro.

## 1916

Edison Medal of the American Institute of Electrical Engineers.

## 1926

Order of St Sava, I Class, awarded by the Government of Yugoslavia.

## 1937

Order of the White Lion, I Class, awarded by the Government of Czechoslovakia.

## 1937

Certificate of Dr Honoris Causa from the University of Paris, France.

## 1939

Honorary Doctor of the University of Sofia, Bulgaria.

UNIVERSITE DE PARIS

Nikola Tesla

UNIVERSITY OF SOFIA

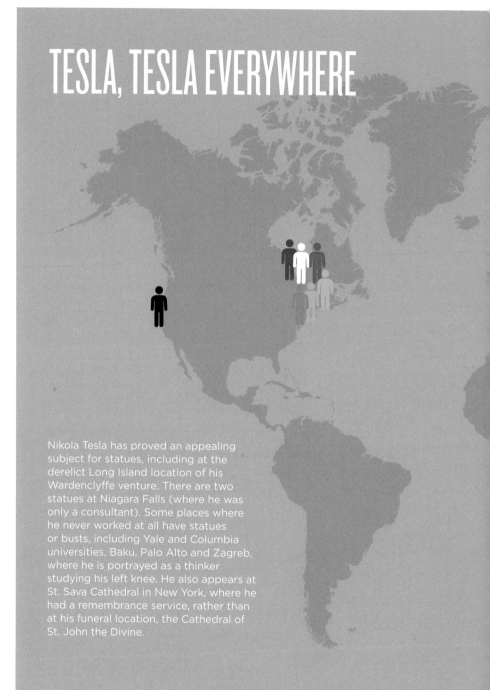

# TESLA, TESLA EVERYWHERE

Nikola Tesla has proved an appealing subject for statues, including at the derelict Long Island location of his Wardenclyffe venture. There are two statues at Niagara Falls (where he was only a consultant). Some places where he never worked at all have statues or busts, including Yale and Columbia universities, Baku, Palo Alto and Zagreb, where he is portrayed as a thinker studying his left knee. He also appears at St. Sava Cathedral in New York, where he had a remembrance service, rather than at his funeral location, the Cathedral of St. John the Divine.

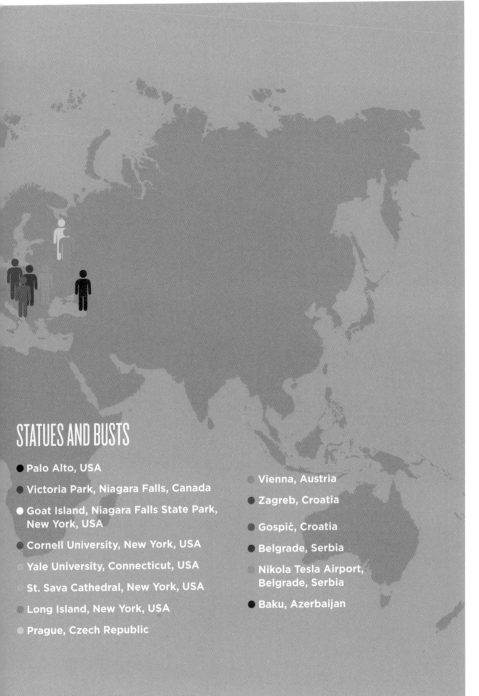

# STATUES AND BUSTS

- Palo Alto, USA
- Victoria Park, Niagara Falls, Canada
- Goat Island, Niagara Falls State Park, New York, USA
- Cornell University, New York, USA
- Yale University, Connecticut, USA
- St. Sava Cathedral, New York, USA
- Long Island, New York, USA
- Prague, Czech Republic

- Vienna, Austria
- Zagreb, Croatia
- Gospić, Croatia
- Belgrade, Serbia
- Nikola Tesla Airport, Belgrade, Serbia
- Baku, Azerbaijan

# THE TESLA MUSEUM

The most extensive collection of material relating to Tesla is in the Nikola Tesla Museum in Belgrade, Serbia, marking his ethnic Serbian origins. The first technical museum in the then Yugoslavia, the building in central Belgrade was originally a grandiose villa, but from 1952 became the home of a Tesla collection – including many original documents and artefacts. After his death, Tesla's equipment and belongings were collected together by the US Office of Alien Property Custodian before being shipped to Belgrade at the instigation of Tesla's heir, his nephew Sava Kosanović. The 60 boxes and trunks formed the core of the museum's exhibits.

**OPENED:**
## 1955

**RECONSTRUCTED:**
## 2006

A model of Tesla's 12-million-volt transformer was built in 2016 in the nearby Kalemegdan Park.

SERBIA

Located in
Belgrade,
Serbia

## MORE THAN 1,200 TECHNICAL EXHIBITS

● = 10 EXHIBITS

## MORE THAN 1,500 PHOTOGRAPHS

■ = 10 EXHIBITS

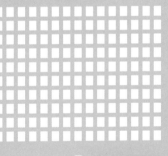

OVER 160,000
ORIGINAL DOCUMENTS

# PYLON MEMORIALS

## 88,000
### PYLONS IN THE UK

Arguably, the most significant memorials to Tesla, reflecting the impact of his work on everyday life, are the electricity pylons (or transmission towers), often carrying high-voltage three-phase AC, that stride across the countryside. While Tesla did not invent AC, he was a leading advocate for its use in electricity generation and his AC motor made its deployment far more acceptable. Ironically, for long-distance transmission, high-voltage DC is now taking over as it loses less energy to heat – most international power supply links, for example, are now high-voltage DC.

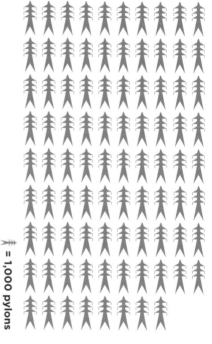

= 1,000 pylons

## TYPES OF PYLON

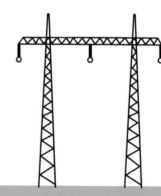
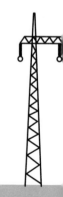

FIR TREE

KEG

PORTAL
(SINGLE)

PORTAL
(DOUBLE)

## WORLD'S TALLEST:

# 1,213ft (370m)

**On Zhoushan Island, China**

## VOLTAGE:
# 500kV

## UK'S SMALLEST:
# 49ft (15m)

# 66kV

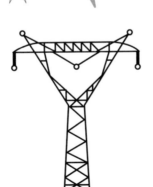

DELTA

CAT

DONAU

# 10 THINGS NAMED AFTER TESLA

## TESLA
### 27-MILE- (43-KM-) WIDE LUNAR CRATER

## 2244 TESLA
### MINOR PLANET

$$T = \frac{V \cdot s}{m^2} = \frac{N}{A \cdot m} = \frac{J}{A \cdot m^2} = \frac{H \cdot A}{m^2} = \frac{Wb}{m^2} = \frac{kg}{C \cdot s} = \frac{N \cdot s}{C \cdot m} = \frac{kg}{A \cdot s^2}$$

## TESLA
### AN SI-DERIVED UNIT OF MAGNETIC FLUX DENSITY (OR MAGNETIC INDUCTIVITY)

## TPP NIKOLA TESLA
### POWER PLANT IN SERBIA

# BELGRADE NIKOLA TESLA AIRPORT

## TESLA MOTORS
### AN ELECTRIC CAR COMPANY

## 128 STREETS IN CROATIA

## TESLA STEM HIGH SCHOOL
### WASHINGTON, USA

## TESLA BANK
### ZAGREB, CROATIA

## TESLA AN AMERICAN HEAVY METAL BAND

# TYPOGRAPHIC TESLA

ELECTRICITY

INVENTION

LABORATORY

PATENT

NIAGARA FALLS

CURRENT

RADIO

TESLA

WESTINGHOUSE

MONUMENT

MOTOR

NEW YORK

TIME

AC

WIRELESS

ELECTRICAL

MORGAN

EDISON

TELEAUTOMATICS

COLORADO SPRINGS

TELEGRAPHY

BELGRADE

WARDENCLYFFE

WAVES

FREQUENCY
MECHANICS
LIGHT
MONEY
TRANSMISSION
NOISSIMSNAGL
EXPERIMENTS
AWARDS
LIGHT BULB
SERBIA
ENGINEERING
INDUCTION MOTOR
TURBINE
ELEPHANT
GENERATOR
NIKOLA
WORLD'S FAIR
CROATIA
ENERGY
PIGEON
DC
SMILJAN
OSCILLATOR
VOLTAGE
ALTERNATING CURRENT
FUTURIST
TESLA COIL

# 21ˢᵗ CENTURY TESLA

If you had typed 'Tesla' into a search engine a few years ago, the results would have been dominated by a whole host of conspiracy websites and offers to sell plans for modern versions of the secret Tesla technology the world never got to see. Now, though, the search results would be dominated by Tesla Inc., Elon Musk's electric car and power storage company. The company was clearly named after Nikola Tesla and, in a sense, is working towards Tesla's dream of being able to transmit electrical energy around the world – though through battery technology rather than broadcast power.

Tesla would have been delighted that, despite using DC batteries, Tesla cars all have AC motors.

Tesla was founded in 2003 by Martin Eberhard and Marc Tarpenning.

Elon Musk joined the company in 2004.

## 13,600,000 ft²
### (1,260,000m²)
**Planned final floor space of Gigafactory 1**

## GIGAFACTORY 1

Built in Nevada, USA, it was the second largest building in the world at the time of construction.

The building is aligned north–south to make it easier for automated equipment to use GPS to navigate it.

Approximate size of a football pitch in comparison

# 100 MW

Power output of world's largest battery in South Australia, launched by Tesla in December 2017

# APRIL 2017

Tesla's market value of $49 billion overtook Ford Motor Company.

# 2.28 SECONDS:

The time a model S takes to get from 0 to 60mph (0 to 97kph) on its fastest setting (Ludicrous mode).

# JUNE 2017

Tesla's market value topped $61 billion, overtaking BMW. As of March 2018, Tesla is yet to make a profit.

## $49 BILLION

## $61 BILLION

# $0

Amount Elon Musk currently banks from Tesla (2018).

# BIOGRAPHIES

**Thomas Commerford Martin**
**(1856–1924)**
Electrical engineer and editor of *Electrical World*, Martin was responsible for much of Tesla's early positive publicity, but later published derogatory articles on his work.

**Milutin Tesla**
**(1819–79)**
Tesla's father, a Serbian Orthodox priest, hoped that Tesla would follow in his footsteps in the priesthood. Their relationship suffered after the death of Tesla's brother.

**John Pierpont Morgan**
**(1837–1913)**
Hugely influential financier and banker Tesla persuaded to invest in his Wardenclyffe broadcast power station. Morgan withheld further funds when nothing practical resulted.

**Anthony Szigeti**
Tesla met Szigeti in Budapest and the two became very close. Szigeti would travel with Tesla first to Paris, then New York. He left abruptly in 1891.

**George Westinghouse**
**(1846–1914)**
It was thanks to Westinghouse's company that Tesla's AC motor was developed to a working device and Tesla received sufficient funds to operate independently.

**Richmond Pearson Hobson**
**(1870–1937)**
A naval officer and politician, Hobson became close friends with Tesla after they were introduced by the Johnsons. Though Hobson later married, they regularly met up.

**Đuka Tesla (1822–92)**
Tesla said he took after his mother who frequently invented things and had a vivid visual memory: he called her "a woman of rare skill and courage".

**Robert Underwood Johnson (1853–1937)**
Writer Johnson and his wife became the closest Tesla had to family in New York. Tesla referred to them as the Filipovs, after a Serbian poem.

**Thomas Edison (1847–1931)**
Edison is often cited as a rival of Tesla's, but if Tesla had not joined the inventor's company in Paris it's unlikely he would have become famous.

**John Jacob Astor IV (1864–1912)**
Wealthy businessman who invested in Tesla's lighting system, though Tesla used the money on his early wireless power research. Died on the RMS *Titanic*.

**Dane Tesla (1848–63)**
Tesla's older brother was killed in a riding accident witnessed by the seven-year-old Tesla. Tesla blamed his obsessions on the changes the trauma wrought in the family.

**Katharine Johnson (1855–1924)**
Robert Johnson's wife was, if anything, even closer to Tesla. She tried to pair Tesla up with a number of female companions, without success.

● family
● friend
● employer
● financier

# INDEX